REFLECTIONS
of
COUNTRY LIFE

REFLECTIONS
of

Country Life

COMPILED BY JOHN HADFIELD

PICTURES FROM THE TATE GALLERY

A GRAHAM TARRANT BOOK

DAVID & CHARLES
Newton Abbot · London · North Pomfret (Vt)

Designed by Julia Alldridge Associates
Cover paper design by courtesy of the Italian Paper Shop, London

British Library Cataloguing in Publication Data

Reflections of country life.
1. Country life—Literature collections
2. English literature
I. Hadfield, John, *1907–*   II. Tate Gallery
820.8′0321734   PR1111.C6

ISBN 0-7153-8855-X

Typeset by Typesetters (Birmingham) Ltd,
Smethwick, West Midlands
and printed in The Netherlands
by Royal Smeets Offset, Weert
for David & Charles Publishers plc
Brunel House   Newton Abbot   Devon

Published in the United States of America
by David & Charles Inc
North Pomfret   Vermont 05053   USA

E NGLAND is a country of gently undulating landscapes, of green
pastures and brown ploughlands where occasionally bare downs and
moorlands break into softer scenes, but where, almost always, rounded
trees and hedgerows continually abound . . . Its landscape is unique among
all landscapes. Other landscapes are humanized like it; but none has its
friendliness, none its satisfying quality of security. Others are merely the
outward settings of human life, the theatres of man's age-old struggle for
existence, the incidental scenes of economic activity. Even where they have
been humanized for thousands of years they still are terrifying though
tamed, still unfriendly though familiarized. They have not yet been brought
to any satisfying human relationship. They may have beauty, but it is of a
stark oppressive quality. Man lives and works there as an infinitesimally
small creature in a vast unbounded space. The scale of those landscapes is
cruelly destructive of man's comfortable self-esteem: reductive of his
stature.

In England the terrifying scale of Nature has been reduced. The
landscape, though it is still the theatre of man's struggle for existence, has
had its distances brought within man's easy comprehension, and is
comfortable and friendly. It is the scene of economic activity, but it has
been given a deeper relationship than that. It has been moulded like a work
of art: it has been given a pattern and a rhythm: it has been made beautiful
through a definite artistic impulse. It is the loveliest, the most humanized of
all landscapes.

THOMAS SHARP
Town and Countryside, 1932

JOHN NASH
The Cornfield, 1918

O VER all the countryside, wherever one goes, indications of techniques are visible to the seeing eye. By technique is meant an exercise of skill acquired by practice and directed to a well foreseen end . . .

The metalled roads tell of it well. The deep-rutted by-roads, too, and the winding lanes, preserve through years of neglect the traces of technique in their hedgerows, however tangled; in their ditches, however choked. On the old ruinous field gate, with its lightly-arched, tapering top bar rudely carved on the under side against the tenon, the grey lichen cannot hide the signs of a vitality of those skilled hands that shaped the timbers. The fields, newly ploughed in straight furrows, or with stubble in long rows, or green lines of wheat just appearing after snow; and the meadows, well rolled and level, or perhaps still wavy from long-forgotten ploughings; and the river banks; and the copses growing up on old 'stamms'; and the woods, thinned out, and full of decayed stumps of felled trees, are all witnesses to the exercise of technical powers, just as are the tools, the farm implements, the waggons and carts, the very horses, and cattle, and sheep. Each detail of country life offers its convincing proof of skill to anyone who cares to look.

GEORGE BOURNE
Lucy Bettesworth, 1913

THOMAS GAINSBOROUGH
The Market Cart, 1786–7

Embrace me then, ye Hills, and close me in:
Now in the clear and open day I feel
Your guardianship; I take it to my heart;
'Tis like the solemn shelter of the night . . .
Nowhere (or is it fancy?) can be found
The one sensation that is here; 'tis here,
Here as it found its way into my heart
In childhood, here as it abides by day,
By night, here only; or in chosen minds
That take it with them hence, where'er they go.
'Tis, but I cannot name it, 'tis the sense
Of majesty, and beauty, and repose,
A blended holiness of earth and sky,
Something that makes this individual spot,
This small abiding-place of many men,
A termination, and a last retreat,
A centre, come from wheresoe'er you will,
A whole without dependence or defect,
Made for itself, and happy in itself,
Perfect contentment, unity entire . . .

WILLIAM WORDSWORTH
The Recluse, 1851 (written 1800)

FRANCIS TOWNE
A View at Ambleside, 1786 (detail)

A landscape of the heart,
Of passion nursed on calm,
Where cloud and stream drew out
His moods, and love became
A brush in his hand, and the elm tree
Lived like a stroke of art.

His sunburst inspiration
Made earthly forms so true
To life, so new to vision,
That now the actual view
Seems a mere phantom, through
Whose blur we glimpse creation . . .

CECIL DAY LEWIS
'Dedham Vale', *Pegasus and Other Poems*, 1957

JOHN CONSTABLE
The Mill Stream, c 1810

O deep unlovely brooklet, moaning slow
  Thro' moorish fen in utter loneliness!
The partridge cowers beside thy loamy flow
  In pulseful tremor, when with sudden press
The huntsman fluskers thro' the rustled heather.
  In March thy sallow-buds from vermeil shells
Break satin-tinted, downy as the feather
  Of moss-chat that among the purplish bells
Breasts into fresh new life her three unborn.
  The plover hovers o'er thee, uttering clear
And mournful-strange, his human cry forlorn:
  While wearily, alone, and void of cheer
Thou guid'st thy nameless waters from the fen,
To sleep unsunned in an untrampled glen.

DAVID GRAY
The Luggie and Other Poems, 1862

JOHN SINGER SARGENT
The Black Brook, 1908

My heart leaps up when I behold
A rainbow in the sky:
So was it when my life began;
So is it now I am a man;
So be it when I shall grow old,
     Or let me die!
The Child is father of the Man;
And I could wish my days to be
Bound each to each by natural piety.

WILLIAM WORDSWORTH
Poems, 1807

J M W TURNER
Buttermere Lake, 1798

His scythe the mower o'er his shoulder leans,
And whetting, jars with sharp and tinkling sound,
Then sweeps again 'mong corn and crackling beans,
And swath by swath flops lengthening o'er the ground;
While 'neath some friendly heap, snug shelter'd round
From spoiling sun, lies hid the heart's delight;
And hearty soaks oft hand the bottle round,
Their toils pursuing with redoubled might –
Great praise to him be due that brought its birth to light.

JOHN CLARE
'The Harvest Morning', *Poems Descriptive of Rural Life and Scenery*, 1820

GEORGE STUBBS
Reapers, 1785 (detail)

Behold her, single in the field,
Yon solitary Highland lass!
Reaping and singing by herself;
Stop here, or gently pass!
Alone she cuts and binds the grain,
And sings a melancholy strain;
O listen! for the Vale profound
Is overflowing with the sound . . .

Will no one tell me what she sings? –
Perhaps the plaintive numbers flow
For old, unhappy, far-off things,
And battles long ago:
Or is it some more humble lay,
Familiar matter of to-day?
Some natural sorrow, loss, or pain,
That has been, and may be again?

Whate'er the theme, the Maiden sang
As if her song could have no ending:
I saw her singing at her work,
And o'er the sickle bending; –
I listened, motionless and still;
And, as I mounted up the hill,
The music in my heart I bore,
Long after it was heard no more.

WILLIAM WORDSWORTH
'The Solitary Reaper', *Poems* 1807

HENRY HERBERT LA THANGUE
The Return of the Reapers, 1886

A NEW field had been thrown open for gleaning and, for the first mile, they walked with some of their school-fellows and their mothers, all very jolly because word had gone round that young Bob Trevor had been on the horse-rake when the field was cleared and had taken good care to leave plenty of good ears behind for the gleaners. 'If the foreman should come nosing round, he's going to tell him that the ra-ake's got a bit out of order and won't clear the stubble proper. But that corner under the two hedges is for his mother. Nobody else is to leaze there.' . . .

The gleaners soon trooped through a gate and dispersed over the stubble, hurrying to stake out their claims. Then Edmund and Laura passed the school and entered on less familiar ground. They were out on their first independent adventure and their hearts thrilled to the new sense of freedom . . . The wagons they met, with names of strange farmers and farms painted across the front, were as exciting as hearing a strange language. A band of long-tailed tits, flitting from bush to bush, a cow or two looking at them over a wall, and the swallows strung out, twittering, along the telegraph wire, made cheerful and satisfying company. But, apart from these, it was not a lonely road, for men were working in the harvest fields on either side and they passed on the road wagons piled high with sheaves and saw other wagons go clattering, empty, back for other loads.

Afterwards they straggled home through the dusk with a corncrake whirring and cockchafers and moths hitting their faces, and saw the lights of the town coming out, one by one, like golden flowers, as they entered. There was no scolding for being late.

FLORA THOMPSON
Over to Candleford, 1941

SIR GEORGE CLAUSEN
The Gleaners Returning, 1908

In this same country as the time fulfilled
When hops like ribands on the maypole frilled
Their colonnaded props mile after mile,
And tattered armies gathered to the spoil,
We too invaded the green arbours ere
The day had glistened on earth's dewy hair,
And through the heat we picked and picked apace,
To fill our half-bin and not lose the chace,
While our bin partner, fierce of eye and tongue,
Disliked our style and gave 'when I was young.'
And all about the clearing setts revealed
The curious colours of the folk afield,
The raven hair, the flamy silk, the blue
Washed purple with all weathers; crime's dark crew;
Babes at the breast; old sailors chewing quids;
And hyacinth eyes beneath soon-dropt eyelids.
The conquest sped, the bramblings, goldings small,
The heavy fuggles to the bins came all,
Garden past garden heard the measurer's horn
Blow truce – advance! until a chillier morn
Saw the last wain load up with pokes and go,
And an empty saddened field looked out below
On trees where smouldered the quick fever-tinge
Of Autumn, on the river's glaucous fringe,
And our own cottage, its far lattice twinkling
Across tired stubble sown with sheep-bells' tinkling.

EDMUND BLUNDEN
'Old Homes', *English Poems*, 1925

WILLIAM DIXON (1800–1820)
Hops

First you shall cut your hay, when grasses stand
In flower, but running not to seed,
But even here rehearse the farmer's creed:
'Tis farmer, not the date, that calls the tune;
Better dry August hay than wet in June.
Have your folks working in the fields by dawn,
Your team of horses doubly spanned;
Leave the cut swath all day; and air by rake
Next morning, and, if weather still be set,
Gather to cocks for carting, but should wet
Flatten the cocks, then you shall tedd and shake
Again when sun returns. Now you shall build
Your rick in yard or field, as suits you best,
Choosing your stacker for a good man skilled,
Building on brushwood, sides both true and straight,
That when hay settles lines may still be plumb;
And let each forkful to its place be pressed
And truly bound, by stacker's treading weight;
Widen your eaving-course; let roof be steep,
Bents sloping outwards, so to keep
Rain from the heart until the thatcher come.
Then you may leave your rick with easy mind;
Fodder for sweet-breathed cattle shall be sweet;
And whether nights be harsh or days be kind
Your hay shall neither moulder, rot, nor heat.

V SACKVILLE-WEST
The Land, 1926

GEORGE STUBBS
Haymakers, 1785

Under a spreading chestnut-tree
  The village smithy stands;
The smith, a mighty man is he
  With large and sinewy hands;
And the muscles of his brawny arms
  Are strong as iron bands . . .

Week in, week out, from morn till night,
  You can hear his bellows blow;
You can hear him swing his heavy sledge,
  With measured beat and slow,
Like a sexton ringing the village bell,
  When the evening sun is low.

And children coming home from school
  Look in at the open door;
They love to see the flaming forge,
  And hear the bellows roar,
And catch the burning sparks that fly
  Like chaff from a threshing floor.

HENRY WADSWORTH LONGFELLOW
'The Village Blacksmith', *Ballads and Other Poems*, 1841

J M W TURNER
A Country Blacksmith, 1807 (detail)

T HE tools were axe and adze and sometimes hand-saw, and the implements (besides a square) a chopping block and a felloe-horse . . . When the simple apparatus had all been got together for one simple-looking process, a never-ending series of variations was introduced by the material. What though two felloes might seem much alike when finished? It was the wheelwright himself who had to make them so. He it was who hewed out that resemblance from quite dissimilar blocks, for no two felloe-blocks were ever alike. Knots here, shakes there, rind-galls, waney edges (edges with more or less of the bark in them), thicknesses, thinnesses, were for ever affording new chances or forbidding previous solutions, whereby a fresh problem confronted the workman's ingenuity every few minutes. He had no band-saw (as now) to drive, with ruthless unintelligence, through every resistance. The timber was far from being a prey, a helpless victim, to a machine. Rather it would lend its own subtle virtues to the man who knew how to humour it: with him, as with an understanding friend, it would co-operate.

So, twisting it, turning it 'end for end', trying it for an inch or two this way and then an inch or two that, a skilful wheel-maker was able to get the best possible product from his timber every time. I don't think I ever afterwards, in the days of band-saws, handled such a large proportion of superlatively good felloes as used to pass through my hands in those days of the axe and adze. Perhaps the sawn-out felloes look better – to a theorist from an office. But at the bench you learn where a hard knot may be even helpful and a wind-shake a source of strength in a felloe; and this was the sort of knowledge that guided the old-fashioned wheelwright's chopping.

GEORGE STURT
The Wheelwright's Shop, 1923

JOHN HILL
The Carpenter's Shop, 1813

THE road . . . during the whole of Easter Monday is in a state of perpetual bustle and noise . . . the dust flies in clouds, ginger-beer corks go off in volleys, the balcony of every public-house is crowded with people, smoking and drinking, half the private houses are turned into tea-shops, fiddles are in great request, every little fruit-shop displays its stall of gilt gingerbread and penny toys; turnpike men are in despair; horses won't go on, and wheels will come off. . . servants-of-all-work, who are not allowed to have followers, and have got a holiday for the day, make the most of their time with the faithful admirer who waits for a stolen interview at the corner of the street every night, when they go to fetch the beer – apprentices grow sentimental, and straw-bonnet makers kind. Everybody is anxious to get on, and actuated by the common wish to be at the fair . . .

CHARLES DICKENS
Sketches by Boz, 1836–7

SIR DAVID WILKIE
The Village Holiday, 1809–11 (detail)

The opening hounds are fired – they snuff and vent,
And trace his footsteps, eager of the scent.
With what prelusive joy they hail the morn,
And with what harmony obey the horn!
Thus roused, away the wakeful savage bounds,
Until his ears have lost the wounding sounds.
Exulting then he takes the distant moor,
And in his cunning thinks himself secure.
A froth besmears his grinning chops around,
And, as he runs along, befoams the ground.
Each hungry dog the lengthening chase pursues,
And snuffs the vapour from the tainted dews;
Till, in united cry, they shoot away,
And in full stretch bear on the bounding prey.
Crowner and Rebel, Kilbuck, Drunkard, Stroler,
Topper and Ringwood, Plowman, Bouncer, Joler;
Vulcan and Thumper, Snowball, Ranter, Gipsy,
Farmer and Steamer, Trueman, Jilter, Tipsy;
Fine-spotted Dainty, Fill-pot, Jewel, Rover,
With long-breath'd Ranger, Dancer, Beauty, Clover,
And many others (all I cannot name),
Still follow, with unequal pace, the game.
With pricked up ears, the hunters then renew
Instinctive courage, and the chase pursue.
Their turgid nerves they swell, they snort and blow,
And whitening foam upon the verdure throw.
The woods, the valleys, and the concave sky,
Both earth and air are filled with harmony . . .

THE REVEREND WETENHALL WILKES
Hounslow Heath, 1747

JOHN NOST SARTORIUS
Fox-Hunting with the Raby Pack: Full Cry, 1804

See! from the brake the whirring pheasant springs,
And mounts exulting on triumphant wings.
Short is his joy; he feels the fiery wound,
Flutters in blood, and panting beats the ground.
Ah! what avail his glossy, varying dyes,
His purple crest, and scarlet-circled eyes,
The vivid green his shining plumes unfold,
His painted wings, and breast that flames with gold?
    Nor yet, when moist Arcturus clouds the sky
The woods and fields their pleasing toils deny.
To plains with well-breath'd beagles we repair,
And trace the mazes of the circling hard.
(Beasts, urg'd by us, their fellow beasts pursue,
And learn of man each other to undo.)
With slaught'ring guns th' unweary'd fowler roves,
When frosts have whiten'd all the naked groves;
Where doves in flocks the leafless trees o'ershade,
And lonely woodcocks haunt the wat'ry glade.
He lifts the tube, and levels with his eye;
Strait a short thunder breaks the frozen sky.
Oft, as in airy rings they skim the heath,
The clam'rous lapwings feel the leaden death;
Oft, as the mounting larks their notes prepare,
They fall, and leave their little lives in air.

ALEXANDER POPE
Windsor Forest, 1713

SIR NATHANIEL DANCE-HOLLAND (1735–1811)
Thomas Nuthall with a Dog and Gun

Hail *Cricket*! glorious, manly, British game!
First of all sports! be first alike in fame!
To my fir'd soul thy busy transports bring,
That I may feel thy raptures while I sing . . .
When the returning sun begins to smile,
And shed its glories round this sea-girt isle;
When new-born nature, deck'd in vivid green,
Chases dull winter from the charming scene,
High panting with delight, the jovial swain
Trips it exulting o'er the flow'r-strew'd plain;
Thy pleasures, *Cricket*! all his heart control,
Thy eager transports dwell upon his soul.
He weighs the well turn'd *Bat's* experienc'd force
And guides the rapid *Ball's* impetuous course:
His supple limbs with nimble labour plies,
Nor bends the grass beneath him as he flies.
The joyous conquests of the late-flown year,
In fancy's paint, with all their charms appear,
And now again he views the long-wish'd season near.

JAMES LOVE
Poems on Several Occasions, 1754

By or after LOUIS PHILIPPE BOITARD
The Cricket Match, 1760

Twiggery, swiggery, shinery, finery, laughery,
  chaffery, pokery, jokery –
Down to the Derby as all of us go,
These are the sights that we each of us know;
Yet off to the Downs as we often have been,
Still every year is some novelty seen . . .

Epsom at last, nearing it fast,
  Smackery, crackery, whip, whip;
There's the Grand Stand, now close at hand,
  Think it a nice little trip, trip.
Get a good view, this one will do,
  Squeezing it, seizing it, rush, rush:
Downs looking smooth, CARELESS's Booth,
  Go in and get a good brush, brush.
Every one here, seems to appear,
  'How d'ye do?' 'How are you?' nod, nod.
Some friends about, can't find 'em out,
  Look for them, hook for them, odd, odd.

Now take your place, this is the race,
  Universe, tune averse, fame, fame;
Cards to be sold, everything told,
  Colours of riders and name, name.
Buzz! off they go, galloping so,
  Bothery, dothery, eye, eye;
Look as they pass, out with the glass,
  Can't find the focus to spy, spy,
Yonder they run, some horse has won,
  Up with the number and see, see;
Whichever is in, hundreds may win,
  But thousands will diddled like me be.

SIR WILLIAM SCHWENK GILBERT
Lost Bab Ballads, 1932 (written c 1875)

WILLIAM POWELL FRITH
The Derby Day, 1856–8 (detail)

THE day ended with a remarkable sunset, even by fen-country standards. The clouds grew like a coral reef on the edge of the world. Particles, sections, layers and shelves of brilliant colours turned the sky into a great wonder. There was no modesty about today's sunset. It was an ostentatious display of theatrical splendour. It heralded a tournament between the day and night. Bright flags of many royal shades were draped across the fields. The clouds shone so much you could *hear* their colours and lesser clouds on the edge of the crowd echoed their fanfares. The space beyond the gaudy array of orange, red, purple and green was a rich bright blue. The sun itself could not be seen but hid, like some great but temperamental actor, in the wings, waiting to make a big entrance or, in this production, a grand exit. People not used to taking much notice of sunsets came out into their gardens or stood at their doors to see the sky burning, to gasp in awe that such things still happened in the world of nature.

EDWARD STOREY
The Solitary Landscape, 1975

J M W TURNER
Sunset on the River, c 1807

With pipe and rural chaunt along,
    The shepherds wind their homeward way,
And with melodious even song,
    Lull to rest the weary day.

Low lies their home 'mongst many a hill,
    In fruitful and deep delved womb;
A little village, safe, and still,
    Where pain and vice full seldom come,
    Nor horrid noise of warlike drum.

There, almost buried from the sight
    Of travellers on the higher ground
Be rushing brooks, and sparkling bright
    Clear, shallow, pebbled streams are found
Where many a fish doth skim and bound.

And intricate with fruit-bent boughs,
    And Flowers, trim cottage gardens are;
And much delight of flocks and herds
    And sweet young maidens passing fair
    The sweetest flowers methinks that are
And Sweeter than the rose beyond compare
And fairer than the milky lilies do appear.

And there's a church-yard something raised
    Above the more unholier ground,
Where swains unnoted, and unpraised,
    In innocent sleep lay sound . . .

SAMUEL PALMER
A poem written in his sketchbook of 1824

SAMUEL PALMER
Coming from Evening Church, 1830

ACKNOWLEDGEMENTS

The publishers gratefully acknowledge permission to reproduce the following
copyright material:

Thomas Sharp,
Town and Countryside (1932)
reprinted by permission of Oxford University Press.

C. Day Lewis,
extract from 'Dedham Vale, Easter 1954', *Pegasus and Other Poems*
reprinted by permission of the Executors of the Estate of C. Day Lewis and A. D. Peters &
Company Limited.

Flora Thompson,
Over to Candleford (1941)
reprinted by permission of Oxford University Press.

Edmund Blunden,
extract from 'Old Homes', *English Poems*
reprinted by permission of A. D. Peters & Company Limited.

Vita Sackville-West,
The Land
reprinted by permission of William Heinemann Limited.

Edward Storey,
Solitary Landscape
reprinted by permission of David Higham Associates Limited.